SIR ASHUTOSH MOOKHERJEA

SIR ASHUTOSH MOOKHERJEA

A CHARACTER STUDY

BY

BIPIN CHANDRA PAL

GYAN

Published by

GYAN

Gyan Publishing House
5, Ansari Road
Daryaganj, New Delhi-110002
Phone: 011-47034999, 9811692060
E-mail: books@gyanbooks.com

Distribution Network
gyanbooks.com
India, USA, Canada, UK, Australia, France

ISBN: 978-81-212-8202-4 (PB)
First Published, 1920

2nd Impression 2023

Printed at: Gyan Press, Delhi.

SIR ASHUTOSH MOOKHERJEA
Author: BIPIN CHANDRA PAL

SIR ASHUTOSH MOOKHERJEA

A CHARACTER STUDY

BY

BIPIN CHANDRA PAL

PUBLISHED BY

DEVA PRASAD DATTA

32, Simla Street, Calcutta.

SIR ASHUTOSH MOOKHERJEA

Sir Ashutosh Mookherjea.

A Character Study.

(Born, Calcutta, June 29, 1864; Father Dr. Gangaprasad Mookherjea, an eminent medical practitioner of Calcutta. Education—Vernacular School, 1869-'72; home education under father 1872-'75; Matriculation (second in the list) 1879; Presidency College, Calcutta, 1880; B.A. 1884 (topping the list); M.A. (Mathematics) 1885; (Physical Science) 1886; Premchand Roychand Student 1886; Fellow Royal Society, Edinburgh, 1886; B.L. 1888; Enrolled Vakil, Calcutta High Court, 1888; Fellow, Calcutta University, 1889; Doctor in Law 1894; University Representative, Bengal Legislative Council, 1899; re-elected, 1901; Bengal Representative (co-opted) Indian Universities' Commission, 1902; Calcutta Corporation Representative, Bengal Legislative Council, 1903; Representative of Non-Official Members of the Bengal Legislative Council in the Imperial Legislative Council, 1903; Judge, Calcutta High Court, from 1904; Vice-Chancellor, Calcutta University, 1906-'14; President, Asiatic Society, Bengal, 1907-'09; President, Indian Museum, 1909; Twice President, Bengal Literary Conference, 1916 and 1919; Member, Calcutta University Commission, 1917-'19.)

A Complex Character.

Sir Ashutosh Mookherjea's is about the most complex public character that I have seen. And it has been my privilege to see, at more or less close quarters, most of the men who have made the religious, social or political history of India during the last half a century. This complexity is, I think, responsible for the widely divergent estimates that diverse people have formed of him. He has enthusiastic admirers, whose admiration often-times verges on fulsome adulation. He has persistent detractors, whose detractions seem sometimes to take the colour of malice. But there is one matter in which both his admirers and detractors seem generally to agree, and it is that he is by far the most powerful public character of his generation.

Men attain power over their fellow-men sometimes through their intellect. Others acquire it through the force of their will. Some gain power through their gift of the tongue, their capacity to rouse and control popular passions. Others gain great influence over their fellow-men through their capacity to please, to instruct and to inspire; all the greatest artists, poets, painters, sculptors, musicians and actors belong to this class. Some gain power through their great wealth or high rank or exalted position. Sir Ashutosh does not fall into any of these classes.

Physical Impression.

Indeed, it seems very doubtful if Sir Ashutosh's personality has ever exercised much influence over his fellow-men. That mysterious quality called personal magnetism is apparently not the greatest asset of his life. This magnetism is, in most cases, a physical quality. And one has only to look at Sir Ashutosh to discover the absence of any suspicion of this physical quality in him. His build is more massive than fine-cut; and though it betokens considerable strength both of body and mind, it is not the subtle strength that draws men near to it, and, by look or gesture, captivates and controls them. He has, no doubt, a pair of large flashing eyes, overhung with bushy eye-brows; and one feels a little uncomfortable when they play upon one's face, as if one's mind and soul were passing through the prism of a spectrum;—but it is very difficult to say whether this feeling is due entirely, if at all, to the gaze of the man or to one's preconceived notions about him as a shrewd judge of human character. A perfect stranger to Sir Ashutosh's public character and reputation can alone answer this question correctly.

In his physical appearance, Sir Ashutosh apparently represents the type, peculiar to the higher classes of Calcutta Hindus—fat, flabby, and delicate. But though fat and flabby, Sir Ashutosh's is by no means a delicate constitution. His extraordinary mental vigour and the enormous amount of work which he has had to put in day after day, as a student, as University Senator and Syndic, as lawyer and legislator, as a judge and the executive head of a large and growing University, and as President of more than one learned Society,—prove extra-ordinary powers of physical endurance, which have been the almost universal foundations of all successful men of affairs. A collection of his Addresses, Literary and Academic—delivered between the years 1907 to 1915, lying before me, covers more than 650 pages of print. A similar collection of his speeches in the Bengal and Imperial Councils would fill as big if not a bigger volume. These addresses and speeches are not mere orations, full of platitudes, padded with common-place facts, copy-book maxims, and cheap rhetoric, with which we are so sickeningly familiar in the Bengal school of oratory, but are fruits of close study, careful observation, and intimate acquaintance with men and affairs. All this would have been impossible unless Sir Ashutosh had been endowed, despite his apparently fat and flabby physique, with very great powers of physical endurance.

Intellectual Type.

It is by no means easy to say how much of Sir Ashutosh's exceptional intellectual powers are part of his original endowment and how much of these is the result of the careful training which he had from his father in the early formative period of his life. That he had considerable native intelligence, the powers of quick perception and incisive analysis, must be admitted; because a plodding intellect could never have helped him to his fairly high position in original mathematical studies and researches, " the substance of which now appears under his name in leading Cambridge text-books." But these high intellectual powers do not constitute the secret of his unique position in our public life. Indeed, his intellect is not exactly of the type that draws and controls fellow-men. Quickness of perception, keenness of analysis, combined with a powerful imagination and persuasive eloquence, constitute the special character of that dominant type. And even the most uncritical of Sir Ashutosh's admirers would not claim for him that powerful imagination or persuasive eloquence which always go to the making of great intellectual leaders. Sir Ashutosh's intellect is of a pre-eminently practical type, that which is quick to seize the relations of men and things, not so much perhaps, in their ideal as in their practical aspects, and which can, almost intuitively, discover the ways and means by which these relations may be moved or worked to some desired practical end. Sir Ashutosh's intellect is of the type that is common to all great political leaders and successful administrators.

Administrator and Politician.

And here we have, I think, what may very well be called the master-key to his complex character. He has been a brilliant student, a successful lawyer and judge, and an eminent educationist. But in all these walks of life, he has only been one among many. In all these, he has had many equals and even some superiors. It is only as Vice-Chancellor of the Calcutta University,—the executive and administrative head of a great and growing institution, that Sir Ashutosh has attained his unique position in our public life. And here, we see in him, above everything else, the capable administrator and politician.

Some people may, however, feel considerable hesitancy in applying the term politician to Sir Ashutosh. In the first place, he is a high official; and no Indian official can be called a politician without offence. Sir Ashutosh has never meddled also in our politics. There have been High Court Judges who stepped to the High Court Bench from the Presidential Chair of the Indian National Congress. Sir Ashutosh is not one of them.

There are other reasons also why one may hesitate to characterize a man of Sir Ashutosh's character and position, as a politician. The word has got a bad odour about it in India. This is largely due to our unfortunate political position. The true politician is more or less out of place in India. There is no room here for the cultivation of those intellectual and moral qualities that make successful politicians in the self-governing countries of the world. Without any pretensions to the democratic ideals, or the high standards of government claimed by the British, even the administration of the Moguls gave us much larger scope for the development of these qualities than what we now have. On the other hand, the British Bureaucrat in India has always been jealous of the position and influence of the independent Indian politician, and has systematically sought to treat him with ill-concealed contempt. The politicians themselves also have been equally responsible for the "degeneration" of this word among us. Few of them have given proofs of any real insight into the actualities of the Indian situation or of any grasp of the larger generalisations of modern-world-politics. Almost all of them have built their political philosophy upon ideas and ideals uncritically borrowed from British history and English literature, and have been trying, all these years, to apply these to their own country, ignoring her different condition and the stage of political evolution which she just now occupies.

This is seen, for instance, in the avidity with which our active politicians seek to secure the help of the State in the promotion of their economic or educational interests, entirely ignoring the obvious fact that state-socialism, in any shape or form, is absolutely unsuited, and positively fatal to countries that have not developed a powerful democracy, where representatives of the people in the national legislature do not exercise complete control over the acts and policies of the executive, and where the interests of the people, as they understand these, have not become the supreme and only concern to their government. Nationalisation of the means of production which must go hand in hand with the nationalisation of the instruments of popular education, cannot *precede*, but must always *follow*, the complete nationalisation or democratisation of the machinery of the government. It has been so in all the great democracies of the West. Until this process of democratisation was fairly complete, the policy of the progressives in all these countries, had been not state socialism, but *laissez faire*. But the copy-book politics of our English-educated classes have no appreciation of these vital political principles; and all this superficiality and imitativeness are very largely responsible for lowering both the standards of political thinking and the character of active politicians among us.

Indeed, the most successful of our politicians have only been very capable debaters. And even here the type has been British. Some quickness of intelligence, some skill in handling or mishandling facts or figures, and a good deal of ready eloquence and effective retort, these are the usual stock-in-trade of the successful Parliamentary debater. We have had one or two of this type among us, whose ability and sweet reasonableness received open recognition from the highest rulers of the land, a recognition that inevitably helped to make their high reputation in the intellectual slave-mart known as respectable opinion in India.

Broadly speaking, however, Indian politicians fall under two classes, the demagogue and the place-hunter; and our political stage is often marked by the exhibition of quick-change artists who change from extremism to moderatism, from violent critics and oponents of the Government to their ardent friend and supporter, with an eye to the ultimate chance of becoming their respected and respectable colleague. In view of all these things, one feels considerable hesitancy in calling Sir Ashutosh a politician. For, he is not a demagogue, and has never been a political place-hunter. At the same time, I know of no other word that can so faithfully sum up his real public character; and I think both friends and foes will agree to accept him as the most clever politician and capable administrator of our generation.

One might, indeed, go further and say that Sir Ashutosh has perhaps been the only politician and administrator that the modern educated Bengalee community has produced. And, considering his achievements in relation to his environments, it may perhaps even be claimed,—not, by any means, in any spirit of petty provincial rivalry, but in perfect truth and justice,—that Sir Ashutosh is the most capable politician and administrator that British India has yet produced.

In claiming this, I do not forget or under-rate the high achievements of men like Sir T. Madhava Rao, or Mr. Rangacharlu or Sir Salar Jung and many others who have made the history of the most progressive of our Native States. But we must not forget the more favourable conditions under which they worked and the comparatively freer hand, which the administrative independence of the States they served, gave them.

Administrator and Statesman.

There is, however, a view of administrative efficiency which measures success only by immediate results. But administrators, who strive only after quick returns, generally make improvident statesmen, who ultimately lead to the political bankruptcy of the State they labour to serve. The vision of far-off ideals, the historic imagination that recognises future possibilities both of good and evil, long before they commence to materialise, and the grasp of the inner psychology of existing actualities, that enable the true statesman to direct present policy with a view to shape the course of future evolution, providing, so far as may be, for the prevention of possible evil and the advancement of possible good,—these are rarely found in the ordinary successful administrator. On the other hand, the grasp of immediate actualities, the sensing of immediate evils, however passing they may be, and the mastery of practical details, that characterise the efficient administrator, are not generally found in combination with far-sighted statesmanship. In practical life, the happiest arrangement, therefore, is to leave the initiation of public policy to people endowed with superior statesmanlike qualities, while the carrying out of this policy may be entrusted to practical men of affairs who have complete mastery of actual details, and are able to work for immediate ends.

It is difficult to say how far, if at all, Sir Ashutosh represents that rare combination of superior statesmanship and high administrative efficiency which have occasionally been found in the great administrators of free countries. His field of work has, so far, been much too limited, his opportunities too few, and even these in a subordinate sphere of public life, to give full play to any high statesmanlike qualities that he may possibly have. This is the universal tragedy of our present public life. One thing, however, is absolutely undeniable. Even the most careless student of Sir Ashutosh's career cannot deny that all appearances and outer impressions to the contrary notwithstanding, he has his visions, like the rest of his educated countrymen and his inner soul is as sensitive to our existing actualities, as the most vocal, or —may I say it without offence—even the most extremist of our patriots and politicians; and that his one aim and intention, in all his public labours, has been, as he himself once declared, to

> Draw new furrows beneath the healthy morn
> And plant the great Here-After in the Now.

As People's Spokesman.

Sir Ashutosh is not the "tribune" of his people, has never aspired to that honour. But, as a member, first of the Bengal Legislative Council, then of the Indian, he has been as loyal and courageous a defender of popular rights as the most agressive of our patriots and politicians. Of course, his style is his own. He never indulged in strong language, and has never appeared on any of our political platforms that offer so much temptation to it. But neither has he trained himself in the courtier's art of saying pleasant things only. His public utterances have always been measured and therefore moderate, in the true sense of the term, but always without any suspicion of falsehood or flattery in them. Sir Ashutosh's speeches both in the Bengal and the Imperial Council would fully bear this out. Discussing certain charges preferred by the Government of India in a letter to the Government of Bengal in connection with the Calcutta Municipal Bill (1899) then before the Council, he said that "Assuming, as indeed it is assumed, in the 13th paragraph of the letter from the Government of India, that the allegation is well-founded, that the existing Corporation has devoted itself to speech rather than to action; assuming further, that in order to check the abuses and anomalies complained of, it is necessary to reduce the numerical strength of the Corporation,"—assuming all this,—Sir Ashutosh declared,—

"It does not necessarily follow that the proposed reduction should be confined to the body of elected Commissioners alone. Indeed, if these positions are granted, and I shall assume for my present purpose that they are granted, it would follow that the reduction should not be confined to the body of elected Commissioners alone, but should be extended to the body of nominated Commissioners as well, unless indeed, the Government is further prepared to affirm that the vice of speech without action is monopolished by the elected Commissioners and the abuses complained of are traceable to them exclusively."

Sir Ashutosh's speech on the motion that the Calcutta Municipal Bill as amended be passed, may be quoted as a very fair example of the style and spirit of his public utterances upon vital questions.—

"I have no desire, Sir, to review at this stage the history and fortune of this legislation. I will not stop, even for a moment, to enquire whether it was wise, whether it was statesman-like, for any Government to introduce into the Council chamber a measure of such magnitude intended to mutilate, if not to destroy, the form of municipal government which has prevailed in the capital of the Indian Empire for well-nigh quarter of a century, till the facts had been ascertained by an independent commission of enquiry in whose decision the public might repose implicit confidence. I will not pause for a moment to enquire whether it was wise, whether it was politic, for any Government to undertake a measure of this character upon an alleged and unproved ground of corruption, which was first publicly formulated in a State document more than twelve months after the Bill had been introduced into the Council. These may not be appropriate subjects of discussion now. But I take it, it is perfectly legitimate to consider whether the

Bill as amended, which in a few moments will become the law of the land does or does not make adequate provision for the removal of the evils to remedy which the Bill was avowedly introduced. One of these so-called evils has been described to be the complete failure of the elective system to secure adequate representation even of the different interests existing in the native city; or, to put it in a more practical and more intelligible form, one of the avowed objects of the Bill was to destroy the dominance of the educated Hindu in the Calcutta Corporation. That object, Sir, I mournfully confess, has been adequately secured by the provisions of this Bill; and I say, with all the emphasis I can command, that the Bill, in so far as it has attained this object, has my unqualified disapproval; in this respect it has not and it cannot have, the smallest measure of my sympathy. But, Sir, it is instructive to enquire, what have you substituted for the dominance of the educated Hindu? You have not satisfied yourself with replacing it by the dominance of the mercantile European or the progressive Mahomedan; but you have replaced it by the irresponsible executive."

. . . .

"But these, Sir, are not the only objectionable features of the Bill. I venture to remind the Council that one of the alleged flagrant abuses to remedy which the promoters of the Bill are so anxious was the growth of party spirit and the appearance among the elected Commissioners of a class of professional and, in some cases, corrupt politicians. I ask, Sir, is there are any provisions in this Bill intended or calculated to remedy these evils, if they really exist. I confess, Sir, I cannot recall to mind any single provision in this direction. On the other hand, I can recall to mind at least one provision which will have the effect of alluring the needy to the Municipal board and of keeping away the honourable who will naturally shrink from a contest which may be construed as a contest for personal gain. I affirm that nothing has been done to remove or to prevent the recurrence of the alleged corruption. You declare that you have discovered a hidden gangrenous sore in a limb of the commonwealth, you refuse to open and examine it, you replace it by a new one, but you provide no guarantee that the sore will not re-appear."

. . . .

"Before I resume my seat, Sir, I desire to take the opportunity of referring to the startling theory propounded this morning by the

Hon'ble Member in charge of this Bill. I have met with some surprises in the course of this prolonged debate, but I did not know that the greatest of these surprises had been reserved for the very last moment. The Hon'ble Member in charge of the Bill has seriously defined the function of this Council to be to carry out the mandate of the Government of the day when the principle of any proposed measure of legislation has been approved by that Government. I would not have been surprised, Sir, if this had been authoritatively laid down to be the duty of the official members of the Council. Thus qualified, I might have left the proposition alone and unchallenged. But I repudiate, in the clearest possible terms, this extraordinary theory when it is applied to non-official members. In spite of the doctrine expounded by the Hon'ble Member-in-charge, I retain, Sir, the right to think and judge for myself. I have made none the custodian of my conscience, and so long as I have the honour of a seat in this Council, it will be my duty to advise the Council to the best of my ability and judgment, regardless of what this or that party may approve or disapprove."

The same style and spirit are equally manifest in Sir Ashutosh's speeches in the Viceroy's Council in 1904 when the Indian Universities Bill was before it. That measure had aroused almost universal antagonism among the politically-minded classes all over India. This antagonism was the bitterest in Bengal, because the conflict between the leaders of the people and the representatives of the Bureaucracy over University affairs was the keenest in Calcutta. Indian politicians judged Lord Curzon's education policy, not by itself, but in the light of his general Indian policy which showed undisguised hostility towards the English-educated classes in the country. Sir Ashutosh's detachment from active politics on the one hand, and his intimate acquaintance with the state of things in the University on the other, helped him to take a more dispassionate view of the Indian Universities Bill than was possible for the general body of his educated countrymen. He was able, therefore, to recognise the good points in that measure. But at the same time he did not hesitate to fight inch by inch the numerous retrograde and reactionary provisions of the Bill and lend his valuable support to the great protagonist of the non-official Indian opposition to these, in the Committee stage, or to record his strong condemnation of these, when the final motion to pass the Bill as amended was brought before the Council.

While dissociating himself "completely from those who maintain that our Universities are ideal institutions and do not stand in need of any reform," he said :—
"I cannot agree with those unfriendly critics who maintain that the Universities have failed in the objects which they have in view, namely, in the words of the great Despatch of 1854—" the diffusion of the improvements, science, philosophy and literature of Europe, in short, of European knowledge,"—and I

cannot but point out that in some quarters at least, the Universities are disliked and cried down, because there is really a dislike of the culture which educated Indians have attained." But though the Universities are not at the present day all that they might or ought to be; the question remains, are the provisions of the present Bill calculated to meet the requirements of the situation?

The provisions of the Bill, broadly speaking, fell into three divisions,—(i) dealing with the relation between the Universities and the affiliated Colleges; (ii) dealing with the constitution of the Universities; and (iii) dealing with the functions of the Universities. With regard to the first of these Sir Ashutosh gave his general support to them, with the reasonable reservation that "there should not be any undue interference with the internal management of the Colleges or with the administration of their finances so long as proper efficiency is maintained." With regard to the second division of the Bill which deals with the constitution of the Universities, he said:—

"My Lord, I wish I could conscientiously say that the constitutional provisions of the Bill are satisfactory and are furnished with the necessary safeguards. Every effort that we have made for securing a statutory recognition of the non-official and of the Indian element on the Senate has been strenuously opposed on behalf of the Government and has consequently failed. I am not one of those who contend that high education must be left entirely to the control of the people. On the other hand, I willingly concede that high education is one of the paramount duties of the State and that it must be nurtured and developed under the fosteding care of a beneficient Government. But I deny most emphatically that it is necessary or desirable to have provisions in the law which may convert the Universities into mere departments of the State. It is quite possible to stunt the growth of a beautiful tree by constant pruning and too affectionate care. I acknowledge with feelings of the sincerest gratitude that the Bill recognises, though to a limited extent, the principle of election, and I hope that at no distant date Government may find it possible to accord it a wider recognition, by throwing open to election a large number of fellowships and conferring the franchise upon professors in our affiliated colleges. But, my Lord, what has caused me the utmost disappointment is the refusal of the Government to define the character of the Senate and to prescribe any statutory rules for the guidance of successive Chancellors; when I add to this the provisions of the Bill which make fellowships terminable after five years, which secure for teachers a position of advantage on the Syndicate by means of artificial rules, which make affiliation and disaffiliation direct acts of the Government and which make it possible, in theory at any rate, for the Government to impose any regulations even on the re-constituted Universities—when I take these together, I feel bound to express my deepest regret that what might otherwise have been a beneficient measure should be disfigured by blemishes of a startling character.

"My Lord, as to one of these particular points of difference I was told that the five years rule was in perfect harmony with the principle which obtains in this country in regard to some of the highest appointments under the State. I was assured, my Lord, that the five years rule works admirably where it prevails. But those who gave me the assurance must have forgotten for the moment a celebrated minute by the late Marquis of Salisbury, dated the 26th of April, 1875, in which the five years rule is condemned in unqualified terms, and it is pointed out that the actions of the Government found a long series of inconsistencies, that it had been found impossible to give permanent force to a new policy and all this was attributed to the fact that "the Indian Government"—my Lord, I will quote the language of the great statesman—"the Indian Government is, by the law of its existence, a government of incessant changes, it is the despotism of a line of kings whose reigns are limited by climatic causes to five years." My Lord, I have quoted the language of one of the greatest British statesman of the nineteenth century and I hope I may be pardoned if I tenaciously adhere to error in such company."

"My Lord, it may be asked why absolute reliance should not be placed upon the capacity of the Government to administer the universities in a perfectly satisfactory manner. Before I answer this question, may I be permitted to point out that education can never be forced upon a people, and that if you want to educate a race you must carry the nation with you. So far at any rate as high education in India is concerned, the policy of the State in recent years has not been quite of the character one would wish......If, however, we examine the history of high education for the last quarter of a century, we shall feel convinced that the condition of things is far from satisfactory. My Lord, the truth of the matter is that we have reached the ebb tide of high education not because the Senates are inefficient, but because the Government has starved its colleges and has weakened its Education Department. ....My Lord, there was a time, not very many years ago, when the Government maintained well-equipped colleges under the management of professors who would be an honour to any University. I am not asking your Excellency to give us illustrious educators of the type of Arnold and Jowett, Kelvin and Ramsay; such personalities are rare even in England and cannot be imported or transported. If, however, Government will give us professors of the type of Professor Cowell, Professor Tawney, Professor Gough, Professor Clarke and Sir John Elliot—I name only a few who are no longer amongst us,—we should have nothing to complain. Each of them was a tower of strength to my University and commanded universal respect and admiration. But, my Lord, we are fallen upon evil times, when safe mediocrity is the order of the day. We are quite familiar with gentlemen who obtain second class or even third class honours at Oxford or at some other English University and are fortunate enough to secure appointments as Professors in Government Colleges in this country. If, upon their arrival. they pose as eminent educational experts and show no unmistakable contempt for their Indian fellow-subjects, who, with all their short-comings, may have devoted years of patient toil to the examination and solution of difficult educational problems, are the latter to be blamed if they show their impatience of these self-constituted experts? My Lord, the real danger in connection with this Bill is that in spite of the best intentions and purest motives of the Government, the actual administration of its provisions may fall into the hands of fifth-rate and unsympathetic teachers, of whom recent events have shown there are not a few in this country, who are uncharitable enough to imagine that the interest in the University which the best among the Indians feel is an interest otherwise than educational. My Lord, I yield to none in my appreciation of the words of the poet—

"And not by Eastern windows only
When day light comes, comes in the light
In front the Sun climes slow, how slowly,
But westward look, the land is bright."

As Patriot.

Relentless criticism of the Government has been the popular standard of sturdy patriotism among us. It would, however, be hardly fair to measure Sir Ashutosh's love for his country and his people only by his measured, but therefore, nonetheless straight and fearless criticism of official acts and policies. Indeed, opportunities for this criticism were closed to him by his appointment as a judge of the Calcutta High Court, almost immediately he had taken his seat in the Imperial Legislative Council. But the whole outlook is radically wrong. Opposition to the Government may proceed from various motives of different or indifferent moral values. The disappointed placeman is an opponent of Government all the world over. In India, social disappointments of Europe-returned gentlemen who wanted to, but could not get admission into Anglo-Indian society, have occasionally ended in suicide; but, more frequently, these have landed the disappointed individual on our political platforms. There have been others, a much more numerous class, whose patriotism has been inspired by alien social and political ideas and whose aim and intention in all their patriotic enterprises have been to emulate British ways and attain British character. In their conduct and conversation they have been British, and Indians only in their opposition to the British officialdom in their country. Intellectual and moral slaves of their foreign masters, they have only aspired to social and political equality with them.

This was, really, the predominant type, in any case in Bengal, before the birth of our new Nationalism at the beginning of the present Christian century.

Sir Ashutosh's patriotism has never been of this type. He is not a disappointed place-man. He easily won the only official position to which he ever aspired. In the days of his youth nothing higher than this was really open to Indian ambitions. The regrettable disturbances in Bengal and elsewhere following upon Lord Curzon's indiscretions, forced the need of drastic reforms upon British statesmanship; and a few high executive offices have since been thrown open to qualified Indians. But Sir Ashutosh's administrative record as Vice-Chancellor of the Calcutta University, has unfortunately offered little encouragement to the Government to take him into their inner counsels. I do not really know, even if high executive office were open to Sir

Ashutosh, whether he would care to exchange the free air of the High Court Bench for the close and, to an Indian conscious of his powers and proud of his own colour and culture, such as Sir Ashutosh undoubtedly is,—painfully stifling atmosphere of the Viceregal Cabinet. If the Government could take courage in both hands and offer him a seat in the Imperial Executive Council, Sir Ashutosh might possibly accept it, not, I believe, from any petty personal consideration, but only to measure strength both of the intellect and will, with the greatest of Anglo-Indian administrators, and prove it to the world, that given adequate opportunities, the Hindu is quite able to hold his own with the cleverest of his political masters, and even to use them as soft clay in the potter's hand. But it is an useless speculation. For, Sir Ashutosh, all his cleverness and diplomacy notwithstanding, has shown his hands too openly in the management of the Calcutta University, to encourage the Government to make any further experiments with him.

Nationalism or Orthodoxy?

To superficial observers, Sir Ashutosh appears as an orthodox Hindu Brahmin whose social and religious ideas and practices cannot be fully reconciled with his intellectual acquirements and the broad outlook that results from modern culture. As a mathematician and scientist, Sir Ashutosh's intellect could not possibly accept the faiths and practices of mediaeval Hinduism as rational. As a diligent student of the psychological group of the sciences, he must know the value of social reform as contributing the necessary dynamic element to social evolution, and cannot possibly be unacquainted with the essentially progressive character of Hindu Society and Hindu civilisation. And, in view of all these things, his unbending orthodoxy would seem to most people as unreal and hypocritical.

I can well understand that Sir Ashutosh would appear so to the Non-conformist, both Christian and Brahmo. But fortunately or unfortunately, Sir Asrutosh does not possess the queer thing known as the Non-conformist Conscience in English life and literature. I do not know what Sir Ashutosh's private religious opinions are, or indeed, if he has any reasoned religious faith at all. But we all know that the usual Hindu *pujahs* are celebrated in his house; and there is no reason to believe that he has no personal participation in these worships. But it is no new thing in India. There is many a Naiyaika and Vedantin, who does not believe in the faiths and practices of the populace, but who acquiesces in these as instruments and agencies of religious and ethical culture in the lower stages of intellectual or spiritual evolution. But, apart from these mediæval apologetics and present practices, even modern thought may well accept these rituals, not as idolatry, as they are interpreted by ignorant or unimaginative critics, but as *ideolatry*, which is the only correct and rational meaning that the history of human faiths and the science of comparative religion, correctly studied and understood, must give to these symbolisms of popular Hinduism. Besides, these Hindu *pujahs* have a variety of aspects through which they appeal to men in various stages of intellectual and moral evolution. To some they appeal through their innate sense of the supernatural which is the universal root and origin of man's religious consciousness. To others these appeal through their artistic sense; while to men with powerful social instincts, these *pujahs* appeal through their social life,—as Christmascelebrations do to most Christians, though, strictly speaking the Christmas, specially among English Protestants, is more of a limited family than a wide social reunion. To the modern-educated Hindu with an inborn religious, a large social, and a cultivated artistic sense, and of wide modern culture, these *pujahs* may well appeal through all these various aspects. And, though not entirely ignorant or forgetful of the evil consequence of too much supernaturalism and symbolism to the human mind and spirit, and their enervating effects upon human character, even the modern-educated Hindu may reasonably accept the popular ceremonialism of his people without any outrage on his reason or his conscience, as the only available symbols and instruments of their present social life and unity.

Apart, however, from these generalisations, that after all may or may not wholly apply to Sir Ashutosh's *personal* religious beliefs, of which I frankly confess complete ignorance,—it is difficult to resist the conclusion that Sir Ashutosh's so-called rigid orthodoxy is a part of his strong nationalism. I use the adjective " so-called " advisedly; because Sir Ashutosh's mental and moral outlook are by no means " orthodox." True it is that he thankfully declined the invitation of Lord Curzon to the Coronation of his late Majesty King Edward VII in London; but his reasons for doing so are not known to the public. They may have been personal, regard for the sentiments of his family, particularly of his old mother for whom he had the deepest love and veneration; they may even possibly have been social, his hesitancy to court social ex-communication. But, I have no doubt, that these, even if they did influence him, must have been only contributory causes of his decision in this matter, the main reason was his strong nationalist instinct. As regards social ex-communication, Sir Ashutosh has braved these things since by the re-marriage of his widowed daughter, which is a much more serious social offence, in the eye of Hindu orthodoxy than "crossing the black waters."

Judging, however, from the general tenor of his life, one may reasonably attribute his refusal to go to England for the late King-Emperor's Coronation, to his determination never to break the social barrier between his people and their present political masters. Sir Ashutosh knows it that once a Hindu is tempted to cross this barrier,—"the protecting line," as the spiritualist calls it, in the relations between the living and the dead, —he loses his claim to real social equality with his political masters, and practically concedes to alien ideals and customs the right to sit in judgment upon national ideals and institutions. There have been orthodox Hindu judges in the Calcutta High Court before and besides Sir Ashutosh. But none of them have so tenaciously held to their national ways, in their relations with the foreign rulers of their country, as Sir Ashutosh seems to have always done. He is rarely seen, outside the precints of the High Court, in his official dress. Even so orthodox a Hindu as the late Sir Gooroodas Banerjea rarely appeared in public, particularly in public meetings where he had to associate with Europeans, in his national dress. But Sir Ashutosh has done so with the utmost unconcern. Even as a member of the Sadler Commission, he never made any change in this matter. Except where official dress was required by long-established official usage, Sir Ashutosh has never, unless for obvious reasons of practical convenience, affected it. At home he sits and works in his "native nakedness"

—which is so sensible a thing to do in our climate,—and has not been known to "change" even when European visitors are announced. These are, apparently, inconsequential little things, possibly due to the necessity imposed upon him by his "flesh" and his climatic environment. But these little things do lend support to the supposition that they may have a deeper origin and meaning, and they may be the outer expression of a profoundly nationalist spirit that resents, and tries to resist, so far as may be, what Mr. Hardayal described as "the social conquest" of India.

Not a Hide-Bound Conservative.

But, whatever may be the real motive or meaning of Sir Ashutosh's so-called orthodoxy, it cannot be said that his social outlook is narrow, or that his sturdy nationalism has helped him to any hide-bound conservatism, as is so frequently found in many of our "orthodox" nationalists. In a remarkable address, delivered before the first Convocation of the University of Mysore, in October, 1918, he declared that while fully admitting that "Indian History, Indian Antiquities, Indian literature, Indian Philosophy, Indian Religion, Indian Mathematics, Indian Astronomy, Indian Medicine, Indian Sociology, Indian Economics, Indian Administration, Indian Art, indeed, all monuments of Indian culture, imperatively demand critical and comparative study in an Indian University," he could "imagine no step more unwise for an Indian University than to give exclusive prominence to studies peculiarly Indian," and entered an emphatic protest against "all suicidal policy of isolation and stagnation."

"Let me ask, what course shall we choose, while the world all round us, is making such gagantic strides on the path of progress, ever seeking to gain mastery over the forces of

Nature? We cannot disentangle ourselves, even if we wish, from irresistible world-currents and sit on the lovely snow-capped peaks of the Himalayas absorbed in contemplation of our glorious past. It is most emphatically true that the community, the people, the nation, the race, which like the Greek philosopher, will live in its own tub and ask the conquering powers around it to move away from its sunshine, will soon be enveloped in eternal darkness, the object of derision for its helplessness and of contempt for its folly. We cannot afford to stand still; we must move or be overwhelmed; we cannot waste precious time and strength in defence of theories and systems which, however valuable in their days, have been swept away by the irresistible avalanche of world-wide changes. We can live neither in nor by the defeated past; and if we would live in the conquering future, we must dedicate our whole strength to shape its course, and our will to discharge its duties. The most pressing question of the hour for the people of every race is, not what they have been hitherto, but what they shall determine to be heretofore; not what their fathers were, but what their children shall be. The past is of value. only in so far as it illuminates the present, the present is of value only in so far as it guides us to shape the future. Let us then raise an emphatic protest against all suicidal policy of isolation and stagnation."

The full significance of this utterance can only be seized when we bear in mind that this was made not before the Calcutta University, with a long past of social revolt and progressive reforms, led by its *alumini;* but before a new University, in a Hindu State, which, all its progressive movements notwithstanding, is still a far more rigid stronghold of Hindu conservatism than any province in British India. Such a declaration, to such an audience, could only proceed from deep conviction.

Broad and Liberal Outlook.

Sir Ashutosh's broad and liberal mental and social outlook is still more pronounced in his Bengalee addresses. These addresses, three in number, were delivered during the last three years, as President of Literary Conferences, and therefore deal mainly with literary topics. But he has always used the word literature in the broadest sense, instead of in the narrow sense of *belles lettres*, in which it is used in Sanskrit and Bengalee; and has discussed the problem of our vernacular literature from the standpoint of our entire social life. The standpoint is essentially modern. To the modern thinker, literature, like every other department of human effort and achievement, is the expression of life. A high literature is only possible in a vigorous social life. Our present social life lacks the vigour and virility of the life of the more progressive societies of our time; and high literary achievements will be impossible unless our society becomes virile and progressive. But literature is also a most powerful instrument of social uplift. And, in the discharge of this essential function, modern Indian literatures must draw their votaries from men who have thoroughly mastered the " improvements, the sciences, the histories and literatures " of the advanced nations of the West.

"If the masses of our people are to be led along the right path—if they are to be helped to attain the full stature of their manhood—if the Bengalee race is to be organised into a great nation, then, means must be found to progressively increase their mental equipments. To do this we must devise means by which the common people, though ignorant of European languages, may yet learn all that is good, pure, and of universal import and application, in the life and literatures of the Western countries, so that they may apply these to the benefit of their own lives and the good of their own society. Whatever is faultless in Western culture, and at the same time is calculated to do us real good,—qualities which, if we are able to acquire them, will be able to add to the existing beauties of our social life and deepen and strengthen our national self-consciousness, must be preached and taught in our own mother tongue to our masses. We are gradually approaching a great crisis in the history of the world, and if we are to hold our own in the fearful competitions of that critical time, we must be fully armed not only with our own familiar native weapons, but must equip ourselves with all the weapons in the improved and rich armoury of the Western nations of our time."—(*Free rendering—Address before the North-Bengal Literary Conference*, 1916.)

But, while nothing must be rejected on the one and all sufficient ground that they are foreign, nor should every thing be preserved simply because they are indigenous to our soil and society.

"I do not say that whatever is foreign is good, and, therefore, must be acceptable to us. I dare not say that whatever is foreign is evil and must, therefore, be summarily rejected as unholy and untouchable by us. When a thing is good, I do not care to enquire if it is *swadeshi* or foreign. Whatever is good must be welcomed, whichever land may claim its origin and growth. Whatever is not free from evil must be renounced, regardless of all considerations as to whether it is mine or any body else's. This is the only simple canon of judgment.

No other canons can be conducive to the good either of our literature or of our society. There may be customs and institutions which, though more or less favourable to social progress in Europe, are entirely unsuited to us, and are likely to work evil in our society. Any attempt to introduce these among us must not only be abortive, but is likely to contribute to the disruption of our well-organised social body."—(*Address before the North-Bengal Literary Conference—free rendering.*)

The ground-work of this liberalism or cosmopolitanism, in the truest sense of the term, is a thorough and critical study of national history, national literature and national ideas of society and civilisation. "Those who do not know what they have, what they had, it is they alone who go a-begging to strangers. Acquint your own countrymen with the acquisitions of your past, analyse those acquisitions and make them realise their value. Quicken the sense of national self-respect in their mind. Then only will it be possible to build up your national life. And the foundations of that life must be laid deep and wide, on a vigorous and expansive national literature."

"Reasonable and discriminating adaptation of the achievements of foreign nations must also contribute to the work of nation-building. Rome built her wonderful life and civilisation by a healthy and helpful assimilation of Greek culture. But Rome had not her own house full of invaluable treasures. Her house was comparatively empty and bare. So, she could greedily take in whatever she found attractive or useful in the life and civilisation of the Greecian people. Our position is, however, entirely different. Our ancient treasures are inexhaustible. Great care and discrimination are, therefore, needed here. We must never take anything from outside which is at all likely to depreciate the value or lower the dignity of our sacred inheritance from the past. At the same time, there are things which we lack, but which foreigners have in abundance; we should never hesitate to take these in, provided always that these do not hurt or prejudice our national life. Our house is not empty and bare, like that of Rome, so that we may any how fill it up. Our house is full. Whatever is calculated to add to the beauty and grandeur of our well-furnished house, whatever is in harmony with the furniture and ornaments of this house, if we find these among others, we must cheerfully acquire and accept them. But that which is not favourable to our national life and evolution—we must never touch."—(*Address before the North-Bengal Literary Conference, free rendering.*)

A Dreamer of Dreams.

Few people would, perhaps, suspect Sir Ashutosh to be obssessed with any exuberant fancies. Indeed, his mathematical and scientific studies, as well his legal profession where he has to deal with solid facts of life, do not give much encouragement to idle fancies. But Sir Ashutosh, like the majority of his educated countrymen, is also a dreamer of dreams. What political dreams he dreams in the solitude of his studies, or in confidential conversations with his intimate friends, the outside public has no means of knowing. As an official of Government, all politics is taboo to him. Even before his " elevation " to the High Court bench, Sir Ashutosh did not throw himself into the mid-currents of our political activities. But there is a very genuine ring of patriotism even in his academic utterances before the Convocations of his University. Addressing the convocation of the Calcutta University in 1913, he declared—" the conviction is deep-rooted in my mind, that India with her great intellectual traditions, India which in olden times was one of the chosen seats of wisdom and learning, is expected, nay, is bound to come to the front rank again and take her place among those nations which are justly regarded as the leaders in the evolution of Humanity in the modern times." But it is in his Bengalee addresses, again, that we recognise the dreamer, the patriot and the idealist in Sir Ashutosh Mukherjea. His vision of the future of Bengalee literature is exalting and inspiring. He believes that " some day Bengalee literature, in the widest sense of the term, will take its place among the most advanced of modern literatures; and, as students of higher Mathematics have now, for instance, to study Russian to get acquainted at first hand, with the works of eminent Russian mathematicians, even so, a time will come when advanced students, whatever their race or country, will have to study the language and literature of Bengal to acquire at first hand correct knowledge of the contributions of Bengalee savants to the common stock of human knowledge and speculations and universal human culture." But all literature is only the expression of life. Sir Ashutosh's dreams of the future of the Bengalee literature, were therefore, inevitably bound up with his deep-rooted conviction that the Bengalee people will also some day claim and secure their rightful place among the most advanced and progressive peoples of the modern world, as an honoured and honorable member of the Federation of Universal Humanity, which is the ideal-end of all human history.

But, Sir Ashutosh's dreams are not mere idle fancies in which so many of our sensitive patriots seek refuge from the cruel actualities of their social and political environments. In fact, his sturdy practical sense would never tolerate any idle fancies. Sir Ashutosh's dreams are really visions of his social ideals; and like the ideals of all trained intelligence, these are rational inductions of what must follow from what is. He sees the seeds of the present in the evolution of the past, and forsees the possibilities of the future in the hidden trends and tendencies of the present. His ideals are, therefore, not wild fancies, but the necessary logic of existing potentialities. Sir Ashutosh has been able to pursue these, progressively, through the instruments and agencies that are within our reach and control. And it is this union of lofty idealism with a strong practical sense that raises Sir Ashutosh from the level of the opportunist practical politician to that of the true statesman.

Constructive Reformer.

Sir Ashutosh's claims to constructive statesmanship of a very high order seem, to my mind, to be fairly established by what he has done in the Calcutta University to secure a recognised position for the Bengalee language and literature in its curriculum.

"It is now nearly twenty-three years ago," (he said addressing the Convocation of his University, held on December 13, 1913, to confer honorary degrees upon Rabindranath and others)—"that a young and inexperienced Member of the Senate earnestly pleaded that a competent knowledge of the vernaculars should be a pre-requisite for admission to a Degree in the Faculty of Arts in this University. The Senators complimented the novice on his eloquence and admired his boldness, but doubted his wisdom, and, by an over-whelming majority, rejected his proposal on what now seems the truly astonishing ground that the

Indian vernaculars did not deserve serious study by Indian students who had entered an Indian University. Fifteen years later, the young Senator, then grown maturer, repeated his efforts with equally disastrous results. In the year following, he was, however, more fortunate and persuaded the Government of Lord Minto to hold that every student in this University should, while still an undergraduate, acquire a competent knowledge of his vernacular and that his profficiency in this respect should be tested precisely in the same manner as in the case of any other branch of knowledge and should be treated as an essential factor of success in his academic career. After a struggle of a quarter of a century, the elementary truth was thus recognised that if the Indian Universities are ever to be indissolubly assimilated with our national life, they must ungrudgingly accord due recognition to the Indian vernaculars. The far-reaching effect of the doctrine thus formulated and accepted, has already begun to manifest itself; but time alone can prove conclusively the beneficient results of this vital and fundamental change."

I cannot say if Sir Ashutosh had in his mind, among the future results of this vital and fundamental change, the institution of a special M. A. Degree in the Faculty of Arts of the Calcutta University in the vernacular literatures of India. It is possible the idea has gradually developed in his mind. And, whether it is the result of his statesmanlike foresight and was at the back of the idea with which he introduced the first reform in this direction, in 1906, or whether he has gradually grown into, or even simply stumbled upon it, no one, perhaps, except Sir Ashutosh himself can definitely say. But the far-reaching import of this reform in our university cannot possibly be ignored. And here one is forced to recognise the constructive statesmanship of the man who has initiated it.

The Problem of Nation-Building in India.

To understand the full import and significance of this new Degree in our University, one must clearly realise the nature of the vital and complex problem of nation-building in modern India. India is not a country but a continent. The Indians are not one people, but are a conglomeration of many communities. They speak many tongues, profess many religions, have diverse usages and customs, own different histories and traditions. All the characteristics of nationhood as known in Europe, are absent here. Judged, therefore, by the common European standard, Indians cannot reasonably lay any claim to it. India had no unity, political, social, linguistic or religious before the establishment of British rule. It has now one Government, and the educated and politically-minded people have found in English a common language for mutual intercourse. The growth of British institutions and the advancement of English or European culture and civilisation will, possibly, on some distant day, work out some sort of an order out of this chaos of many languages, many religions, many social economies, and many customs and traditions of this heterogenous mass of Indian humanity. This is the popular British and bureaucratic view. I am not sure that a good many of our own "sensible and saner" politicians of the type, for instance, of Baron Satyendra Prasanna Sinha, do not largely share this view. If the assumptions at the back of it be true, then we must start cultivating the patience of Job, with a view to the peaceful evolution of modern national life and democratic institutions among us.

A correct study and appreciation of Indian history, however, encourage an altogether different view. The definition of nationhood in Europe is the generalisation of European experience, of Europen history and evolution only. These generalisations are absolutely inapplicable to India with a different history and evolution. Hinduism is not one religion, like Christianity or Islam, or even Buddhism, all of which are classed as credal, but a federation of many doctrines, dogmas, cults and disciplines, many authorities, scriptural and personal (the authority of the *Guru* for instance),—and many theological and philosophical systems and speculations. Hindu society is also a federation of many castes and communities, each autonomous within itself, but joined to others in common subjection to a general, but not uniform, social law and order. In view of all this, the particular type of nationhood developed in India has been fundamentally different, both in ideal and structure, from the European type. National unity in India was not secured, as in Europe, by the more or less complete elimination of all vital differences between one community or society and another, but by working out a federation between diverse communities and cultures, standing in different stages of evolution. The fundamental unity of the Indian peoples was not political, as that of the nations of Europe, but cultural.

The emphasis of the ancient Greeco-Roman culture in Europe, out of which the modern European culture has evolved, was on their state-life. The State was the sign and symbol of their Social Whole. Consequently, every other department of life,—religious, moral, æsthetic,—was subordinate to and subsumed in the life of the State. Even the gods formed a part of it, and their worship was enforced by the authority of the State. Christianity spread in Europe only after it was identified with the State, through the conversion of Constantine; and latterly the Rome of the Popes became the centre of European life and culture, by its secret alliances with, and assumption of authority over, the heads of political society in

Christendom. Even to this day, European life and society are dominated by political ideals and controlled by political authority. Nationhood in Europe is, therefore, an essentially political fact.

But India followed a different course of evolution. Indian unity was never political, but cultural. The Hindu bound together the diverse races and peoples of India into one communion or community, neither through their conversion to a common credal religion, nor through their subjection to a common State or political authority, but through the inculcation of a common culture among them. The ancient Hindu nation-builder recognised the freedom of other cultures, respected the sanctity of other faiths, and tolerated all diversities and differences; all that he did was to give these diversities and differences a place in a general social scheme, usually known as *Varnasrama Dharma* or the law of caste-and-order; and to accomodate diverse gods and cults inside a wide socio-religious federation. He respected and gave room for the completest freedom of the units inside the unity of a great organic whole. From of old India developed, thus, a new type of nationhood, entirely different from, and absolutely unknown to, European history and experience. This fundamental peculiarity of Indian history and culture must never be overlooked by the modern nation-builder in India. The problem of Indian unity cán hope for a rational solution, consistent with Indian tradition and Indian character, and without destroying the regulative idea that has hitherto controlled Indian social evolution, only from those who will not ignore this fundamental peculiarity of Indian history.

I cannot say if there is any clear ennuciation of this problem in any of Sir Ashutosh's writings and speeches. I have not seen it as yet anywhere. But I cannot refuse to admit that though others have put forward this peculiarity of Indian culture and history as evidence of the development of a special type of nation-hood in India; not only different from, but in view of its more complex and organic character, even superior to, the European type, none of them, so far as I know, has indicated the practical method of its preservation and advancement under modern conditions, as Sir Ashutosh has undoubtedly done.

In ancient and mediæval times, federation of the different races and peoples of India was worked upon a socio-religious basis; because, the emphasis of the life and thought of those times was distinctly religious and social. It would be obviously foolish, and even positively suicidal, to attempt any reconstruction of Indian unity upon the old socio-religious bases. The old social authority is dead. The old social order is decadent. The old religious faiths have lost their reality. Neither the Vedas, nor the *Varnasrama* can build up the unity of India in our time. We have to deal not with Hindus only, but with Mahomedans and Christians, who have their own scriptures and their own socio-religious institutions. We cannot take them in, in any scheme of "re-interpretation, re-explanation, restatement and re-adjustment" of Hindu faiths, practices, and institutions, that may be made to meet the requirements of modern life and thought. We cannot leave the non-Hindu out of any scheme of national reconstruction in modern India. Raja Ram Mohan foresaw all this; and, therefore, sought to solve this problem, through the institution of a liberal school of religious thought and a common House of Prayer, which came to be known as the Brahmo Samaj. But even in the Raja's scheme, the emphasis is clearly on religion, though he did add works of public utility —of what he called *loka-shreya*, to it. But since then much water has flown along the Hooghly; and no one would think of reviving the form of the Raja's solution of this problem in our time. I use the word " form " advisedly; because the spirit of the solution tried by Raja Ram Mohan seems to be fully present in that of Sir Ashutosh.

The evolution of federal nationality was in its early unconscious stage in ancient and mediæval India. We have long passed that unconscious stage. The peculiar environments of Indian society, and the particular historic epoch through which it was passing in those times, forced this line of evolution upon the ancients. But our environments are not the same. Our epoch is different. We can either lifelessly and thoughtlessly drift along the new currents, and resign our future to chance; or we can raise ourselves to the plane of an ever-wakeful national consciousness, and help to shape the course of our future with our wisdom and our foresight, and our unbending determination to ride on, and not fall under, the wheel of modern civilisation which, like the Car of Jagannath has commenced already to move among us. And in the institution of the new M.A. degree in the Indian vernaculars, Sir Ashutosh has indicated the line, along which we can move immediately towards the solution of the vital problem of Indian unity and federation in our time. While some of us had long recognised the federal and cultural type of ancient Indian nation-hood, it is Sir Ashutosh who has, for the first time, so far as I know, indicated the line along which alone can this peculiarly Indian type of nationality be practically preserved and developed in modern India.

Lord Hardinge had indicated the political ideal of British India, as a federation of provincial autonomies, controlled by a Central Government, the Government of India. But there are possible dangers to national unity in India in the fullest and freest development of these provincial autonomies. The provinces are large in area and population, and command sufficient natural resources, to be tempted to bid for sovereign independence. Bengal, Bombay, Madras and Sindh have extensive sea-boards which will justify the building of provincial navies. Lord Hardinge evidently realised these possibilities, and, therefore, he would not weaken the authority, or alter the character of the Imperial or Central Government, even though His Excellency threw out the ideal of a United States of India. Mr. Lionel Curtis, on the other hand, from sensing the same possibilities, has been for the cutting up of our larger provinces into a number of smaller ones. These are the only devices that the mere politician could think of, to provide against the possible disruption of Indian unity in consequence of any real development of provincial autonomy in the country.

But these cannot appeal to any Indian Nationalist. He cannot consent to any scheme which will perpetuate the autocratic character of the present Central Government of India. No scheme of constitutional reforms can be satisfactory and acceptable to Indian Nationalism which will not give a truly federal character to the Government of India and make it responsible to the representatives of the different states or provinces in the Indian Union. Nor is it possible to destroy the unity and individuality of the different provinces; because this unity and individuality is the growth of countless centuries and has at its back immemorial traditions, long-established usages, special social economies, religious institutions, ancient history and literature. Bengal, Madras, Bombay, Sindh and the Punjab are different from one another as are the existing States of the European Continent. No more can we dismember Bengal, or Maharastra, or the Tamil and the Telugu countries for the sake of Indian unity, than we can dismember the Anglo-Saxon, or the Slavonic or the Latin or Teutonic States of Europe for the promotion of European unity. The provinces must be preserved intact, full autonomy must be secured for every province, the autocracy and irresponsibility of Central Government of India must be removed, and, at the same time, the foundations of Indian unity, which is based at present upon subjection to a common political authority, autocratic in its character and therefore able to impose its will upon all; and invincible in its strength, and therefore able to check and crush all tendencies to break out in revolt;—must be maintained. This is the real problem before us. And in laying the foundations of an All-India Literature, Sir Ashutosh has indicated, at least, one of the ways along which we must seek its solution.

This ideal of an All-India Literature is the theme of his latest address (1919) as President of the last Bengal Literary Conference. This All-India Literature will not speak in any particular tongue, all the vernaculars of India will be its vehicle. " It will not secure unity of language," but certainly the more vital. " unity of thought and culture." For, though speaking in diverse tongues, it will express the same thoughts and breathe the same aspirations, formulate the same ideas and ideals, and thus once more re-establish that fundamental cultural unity of India which expressed itself in ancient and mediæval times, through religious formulas and social moulds. The recent regulation of the Calcutta University, instituting the M.A. Degree in the Vernacular Languages of India, in the Faculty of Arts, has opened the way to the building up of this All-India Literature.

The popular view that Sir Ashutosh has instituted a new degree in Bengalee is entirely wrong. Those who appear for the M.A. Degree in English have to study English language and literature only. But those who will seek the M.A. Degree in Bengalee will have to read up at least one other modern Indian language and literature, whether it be Hindi or Mahrati, or Guzrati, or Telugu, or Tamil or Urdu. Those who take this new Degree in our University will, at least some of them, be able to work as medium of communication between the higher thought of Bengal and the other Indian provinces. At present we have, no doubt, in the English language, a medium of inter-provincial thought-communication. But the masses do not, and cannot, partake of the benefit of this intellectual exchange-mart. "Yet it is they who form the Real India." They are innocent of English. Indian unity can only mean the unity of the Indian masses, and not the unity of a mere handful of English-educated Indians. If we are to work up a real cultural unity in India, we must help the masses to understand, to appreciate, to enjoy and assimilate this great Indian Culture. And the first step in this direction has been taken by the Calcutta University in the institution of this new Degree, which raises Sir Ashutosh's claim from that of a clever and successful administrator to that of a constructive statesman, with as clear a vision of the future as he has a strong grasp of the present.

Achirvements in the "New University."

I have already overstepped the limits of this study, and cannot deal here in detail, with Sir Ashutosh's work and achievement in the Calcutta University. The story of Lord Curzon's University-reform in India has not as yet been clearly told. English educationists cannot, therefore, really understand why the endeavours in this direction of the one man who has done so much for the reform of his own University at Oxford and has proved his exceptional abilities there, should have roused so much opposition from the educated classes in India. This question can only be answered by a clear exposition of the different aim and intention, that differently actuated the reformer in the two cases. In Oxford, Lord

Curzon was purely an educationist, working with single-minded devotion for purely intellectual and cultural ends. In India, Lord Curzon was not merely an educationist, but also a ruler responsible for the protection of the political and economic interests of the British people and the preservation of British suzerainty. Here his educational aims were necessarily subordinate to his political aims. Education was not here an end unto itself. In any case, rightly or wrongly, people believed that Lord Curzon's education reforms in India had for their objective the creation of an Indian mentality that would acquiesce in the present political subjection of the people, and accept it even as a god-send. In a word, not the development of a virile manhood, but the manufacture of "loyal citizens" was generally believed to be the main object of these reforms. This view found expression even in the Imperial Legislative

Council when the Indian Universities' Bill was before it and Hon'ble Members frankly said that its practical result would be to convert the Universities into Departments of the Executive Government. That view has been partly justified by the action and attitude of the Government of India in more than one instance, in their dealings with the Calcutta University. But on the whole, however, that object has practically failed; and the credit of this failure, so far as the Calcutta University is concerned, is entirely due to the very high administrative qualities and diplomatic management of Sir Ashutosh, as the first Vice-Chancellor, on whom devoted the carrying out of the provisions of the New University Act. But a detailed consideration of Sir Ashutosh's work and achievements in the University must be left for the future when the organisations now in progress are completed and the whole scheme of his University reforms has had time to mature and justify itself. I will content myself, for the present, by simply quoting his own pronouncement upon the work that he and others associated with him had done during the eight years, 1906-1914, that Sir Ashutosh was Vice-Chancellor of our University. In his last Convocation Address as Vice-Chancellor (March 28, 1914), he said :—

"The joy and pride to which I confess are not, however, all unmixed. I too vividly remember, I too intensely feel the after-effects of all the struggles we had to pass through before the accomplishment of our aims, not to feel at times seriously anxious as to the future of what I may call the New University. Though much has been done, more remains to be done, and who knows what the future may bring. I at times truly feel like the careworn toiler of the soil, when on fields first brought under the plough by him, he at last sees the earliest tender green shoots issue from the ground. He dwells in remembrance on the long series of hard labours he had to undergo in order to carry things so far—the felling of trees, the digging out of stubborn roots and stones, the draining of marshy soil, the clearing of obstructive weeds, and then finally the toils of ploughing and sowing. Now, at last, the first fruits of all this labour begin to show themselves, refreshing his eyes and gladdening his heart. But yet, how much may not intervene before full fruition is obtained, before, from the delicate emerald shoots there have risen the serried ranks of ripe ears, each of them proudly balancing at the top its little treasury of golden grains, and, again, how much may not happen before all those precious grains have been safely gathered and stored in barns, ready to supply wholesome food to the cultivator, for his family, for his tribe. Untimely drought may wither the young stalks, storms and rain may beat down the ears, fierce hail may lacerate them, noxious insects may destroy the ripening grain. The cultivator has done his best; he now stands helpless; nothing is left to him, but to hope, to pray and to trust. I repeat, I at times feel like that toiler of the fields.

I too, or let me rather say, we too—I and my helpers—have worked in the sweat of our brows; have spent laborious days and anxious nights; we too have hoped for a glorious harvest, a harvest not palpable, but not the less real on that acount, a harvest in the fields of the spirit and the intellect, supplying nourishment which a great people needs, no less than wholesome material bread, pure water, pure atmosphere. We have prepared the ground and now see the first fruit of our labour. But here also how much may not happen to prevent the full ripening of the harvest. I must admit when I recall to memory all the difficulties it gave us such heavy trouble to overcome, and when I picture to myself in my imagination all the difficulties that may beset the future path of the University, I have moments of deep anxiety. The steady opposition which we had to face is not yet crushed, and it is all the more dangerous when it chooses to move in the dark. Sympathy has failed in quarters where we had a right to demand it, and where we confidently reckoned on it. But more even then well-defined opposition and clearly declared want of sympathy, I dread want of fortitude and energy on the part of those who at the bottom view our efforts with approbation. I dread pusillanimity which shrinks at the first rough collision with determined hostility, that cowardly spirit of compromise which often induces a weak man to accept a fraction of the reward for which he has hitherto contended, while one resolute step in advance, one bold thrust of the arm, might have secured for him the whole glorious prize. All these dangers are vividly realised, and hence my feelings are sometimes not unlike those of the husbandman when he sees dark clouds massing on the horizon and hears the muffled sound of distant thunder. To me also, nothing is left but to hope, to pray, to trust.

But, far be it from me to close this address of mine with a note of fear and despondency. The spectres of doubt and apprehension which crowd round the bravest even, vanish into nothingness when faced with resolution. When all is said and done, there is alive in the depths of my soul the unshakable conviction that I and my helpers have, during these last years, fought a good fight; that the light, which has kept beckoning us onward on our rough and dark path, was not the fitful gleam of a will-o'-the-wisp, but the steady radiance of a pure and holy flame for ever burning in a glorious temple, however far remote,—a shrine dedicated to the True and the Ideal. Let us, therefore, advance, the banner of progress in hand, with bold but not unwary steps, drawing confidence and inspiration from the consciousness that so many of the best and truest men of our people are in full sympathy with us, that the rising generation has availed itself with eagerness, nay enthusiasm, of the new opportunities we have created for higher studies; that the spark of the new inextinguishable fire kindled in our midst have already leapt to all parts of India, and that the Sister Universities are eager to imitate and emulate what we have boldly initiated. I feel that a mighty new spirit has been aroused, a spirit that will not be quenched; and this conviction, indeed, is a deep comfort to me at the moment when I take leave from work dear to me for so many weighty reasons. The workers pass away; the solid results of their work remain and fructify. I thus bid farewell to office and fellow-workers, not without anxiety for the future of my University, but yet with a great measure of inward contentment: and—let this be my last word—from the depths of my soul, there arises a fervent prayer for the perennial welfare of our Alma Mater—for whom it was given to me to do much work and suffer to some extent—and of that greater parental Divinity to whom even our great University is a mere hand-maiden as it were—my beloved Motherland."

Light and Shade.

Sir Ashutosh like all men, has the

faults of his exceptional intellectual and moral qualities. The greatest of these, his detractors constantly remind us, is his weakness for doing all things himself and giving little room for the growth of initiative and independence in those with whom he has to work, and the autocracy and one-man-rule, which it inevitably leads to. That there is a great deal of truth in this indictment, if indictment it at all be, cannot perhaps be denied. But no one except his most intimate personal friends can say, how far or how much of this autocracy is temperamental and how much of it is the result of the peculiar conditions under which he has had to work.

It is absolutely clear that Sir Ashutosh accepted the Vice-Chancellorship of the Calcutta University at a time when it was really threatened with the prospect of being converted into a department of the Government of India. The forces ranged against those who were anxious to preserve the legitimate freedom of the University were almost overwhelming. They were, practically, the forces of the Government Education Department and their allies in the non-Indian colleges within the University. In the active members of the earlier Senates with whom Sir Ashutosh had to work, there was an overwhelming majority of officials and European non-officials; and to organise the forces of progress out of such a body was no easy task. And the necessity of fighting his battles with a numerically weaker army, necessarily called for considerable discipline, which inevitably developed autocratic tendency in the leader. As a clever general uses and applies all the well-known methods of discipline and strategy, to keep his forces together and weaken those of the enemy, even so Sir Ashutosh has had to do. He was forced by the necessity of the situation to strengthen support and weaken opposition by judicious distribution of patronage. All these things cannot be done without laying one's self open to charges of favouritism and partiality. As an administrator, called upon to make bricks almost without straw, Sir Ashutosh could not afford the luxury of what is called the Non-conformist conscience, which repels all compromises as sinful. All this must be taken into account while passing judgment upon his policy and acts. But why should not even his friends admit his weaknesses either. Those who have large patronage at their disposal may sometimes be tempted to misuse it. If Sir Ashutosh has occasionally succumbed to this temptation, it only proves that, however great he may be, indeed undeniably is, as an administrator and statesman, he has the common failings of common men, which in no way take away from his universally-admitted endowments and acquisitions, or weaken his claim to be counted among the most capable administrators and statesmen that British India has as yet produced.

The Future.

In four or five years time, Sir Ashutosh will gain his freedom from office. A man of his temperament and habit will not find it possible to live the rest of his days in peaceful retirement. Indeed, to judge from his recent public activities, one is encouraged to think that Sir Ashutosh will, on his release from office, join the advanced Indian political platform. Then will, I fear, come the real trial of his life. For, here he will have to work out the apparently hopeless problem of organising as an effective fighting force the growing democracy of educated India, and of reconciling the discipline of constitutional political agitation, with the freedom of thought, speech, and action, of an assembly like the Indian National Congress. Perhaps, he will succeed. Perhaps, he will fail. It is not yet possible to foresee that future. Let us wait, perhaps with mixed feelings of hope and fear, and see.